TEENAGE PET GUNDOG FIREWORK SURVIVAL GUIDE

HOW TO STOP YOUR GUNDOG FROM BEING SCARED OF FIREWORKS

BY HARRIET GOODALL

Published by WriterMotive
www.writermotive.com

In Loving Memory of Barney

Miss you 'Wiggle Bum' x

Praise for 'Teenage Pet Gundog Survival Guide'
What dog owners are saying about ' *Teenage Pet Gundog Survival Guide'*

"Harriet's knowledge and love of gundogs shine through in this short but meaty book. She tells you how to help your dog if they are frightened of fireworks and gives you a simple ten-point plan to follow. She also describes several ways to help prevent your dog from having a meltdown next year by giving you sound, sensible advice on how to desensitise them to those scary noises in future. Harriet also gives you some excellent bonus games to play, which will challenge and tire your gundog at home. Harriet writes with humour and wit, and it is an enjoyable read, as well as being packed with useful information. Well done, Harriet, on writing a fantastic first book."

Carol Clark – 'The Doggy Doctor
https://www.downdog.co.uk/

"This book is just brilliant. It's full of practical and easy to follow advice on how to help your dog during firework season and also explains how your dog is thinking and feeling in a way that is easy to understand and not patronising. I loved the stories from Harriet about her granddad and her daughter, Scarlett, and the funny anecdotes about her dogs. Especially Finn pinching the Yorkshire puds. There is so much brilliant advice in her about fireworks and understanding and caring for your dog all year round."

Rachel Spencer – Pet publicity specialist
www.thepawpost.co.uk
https://www.publicityforpetbusinesses.co.uk/

"A must-have book for anyone trying to train their dog to be calm on those dreaded fireworks nights. All the information you could possibly need laid out with real-life quips intertwined that we can all relate to."
Steve Catt

"A brilliantly written book with delightful stories we can all relate to and all the information necessary needed to get your dogs and yourselves through the stressful firework nights."
Lesley Kirk

What some of my clients have to say about my 1-2-1 training sessions

"Lucky has come on leaps and bounds since our 1st meeting & looking forward to our next two already booked. Professional, friendly & great service." **Stephen Massey and Lucky**

"Harriet is a great trainer, very friendly and professional. Loki (our Springer) is grateful for all the help!" **Omer, Su, Ela Kirdar and Loki**

"Harriet Goodall is a true dog lover and a great trainer. I highly recommend her and her service. Her advice has been so helpful with our puppy." **Brian Leiser and Lola**

"Harriet is great – very skilled and knowledgable – and also very understanding – able to tailor her advice to my circumstances and help massively with our puppy's recall – highly recommended." **Stephanie Daley and Nancy**

"Harriet came and observed the dogs. She asked questions and then suggested reasons for the various behaviours they were exhibiting. She accompanied me on a walk with both dogs in turn and taught me how to stop their pulling. They reacted immediately. We have two more sessions booked, and after the first, we got a written plan." **Louise, Max and Scout Charlesworth**

"Totally recommend Harriet! She did a session with our teenager a week ago, and we are noticing improvement already" **Eric Horrell & Terri Townsley & Max**

Contents

Introduction

There are many great things about autumn that we wait all year for, such as cosy evenings drinking hot chocolate, Strictly Come Dancing, hearing the crisp sound of dried leaves under our feet and not forgetting the Great British Bake-off.

If you have a gundog that is scared of fireworks, you probably won't be able to enjoy any of this above, well not peacefully anyway.

You have to witness your beloved pet in distress, and you feel frustrated and powerless that you can't make it better.

If it were only for a few days during the year, you and your pet gundog might be able to live with it. But nowadays, fireworks are used pretty much all year around to celebrate occasions such as New Year's Day, Diwali, Chinese New Year and Bonfire night.

People love to wrap up warm with scarves and woolly hats and head out with loved ones to 'ooh and 'aaah' at the colourful displays.

When I was a child, my grandad would have firework displays in his garden. He would cook us a yummy barbecue of burgers and sausages—the perfect food for a cold night around the bonfire.

Once, he offered me a black banana that he cooked on the barbecue, I pulled a face and politely said 'no thank you' and wondered why the hell he has offered me a rotten banana.

Apparently, you can stuff them, and it's a traditional bonfire food. I prefer my bananas yellow and with ice cream, chocolate sauce, squinty cream and nuts. Otherwise known as drum roll please - banana split.

I wasn't really bothered about fireworks. I couldn't see what all the fuss was about. I did enjoy holding the sparklers and moving them in circles to create pretty patterns, but that was about it.

At most family celebrations, you would normally find me wherever the animals were. Bonfire night was no exception. I was always cuddled up on the sofa with my grandad's dog, Crystal, on my lap. Thankfully, she wasn't bothered about the fireworks either.

It is a very different story for those dogs and their owners that dread the firework season.

It would be acceptable if the fireworks just went off on Bonfire night, but they go off every night or even a month before, so it makes it really difficult for us to prepare our dogs for the evening ahead.

The legislation governing fireworks in the U.K. is contained in The Fireworks Regulations 2004. The current law says ' *you must not set off or throw fireworks, including sparkles in the street or other public places. You must not set off fireworks between 11am and 7pm. Bonfire night cut off is midnight and New year eve the cut off is 1am.*

I don't want to be the fun police. Personally, I think it is complete insanity that members of the public are allowed to buy explosives and detonate them in residential areas.

Bonfire night is traditionally one of the busiest nights for the London Fire Brigade. There are many incidents, no matter the day that it falls on. In 2018, the London Fire Brigade attended more than 900 incidents over the Halloween and Bonfire night period.

London fire brigade warns *'Fireworks can be spectacular, but they are explosives and can cause serious injury if handled irresponsibly. A hospital visit or damage to your home will make you remember November 5, but for all the wrong reasons'.*

I fully understand that some people find the spectacle of fireworks an enjoyable experience. And I'm not suggesting that they should be banned completely.

I do, however, think that improvements could be made to the current legislation in order to better protect animals and restrict the use of fireworks to professional, organised events only.

How about getting rid of the loud bangs and replacing them with low noise fireworks. Like Aurora Fireworks, a company in Billinghurst, West Sussex, that has colourful displays for those that enjoy them whilst avoiding the excessive noise that is so stressful for animals

In recent years, there have been many petitions about banning the sale of fireworks to the general public, and also, in 2019, Sainsbury's announced they would not be selling fireworks in their stores.

There is some progress, but unless legislation changes, we will still have to watch our pets in distress.

Although, it doesn't need to be like that. That's why I decided to write this book. I wanted to help dogs, and their owners have a calm and comfortable evening during fireworks season.

'Teenage Pet Gundog Teenage Firework Survival guide' is book one of the *Teenage Pet Gundog series.* This series will be full of simple, helpful and entertaining information that you can go away with and transform your dog's behaviour.

Throughout the book, I will be talking about mostly three dogs with three different reactions to fireworks, so I thought it would be good for you to get to know them.

Please allow me to introduce you to Barney, at the time of writing this, he is eleven years old. He is a yellow Labrador. This is the dog that made me fall in love with Gundogs. Every time I come through the front door, he always does the Labrador bum wiggle (Labrador owners, you know what I mean).

Jake is about eight years old; my parents adopted him from a rescue centre in Ireland. We think he is a German Shepherd cross with a Belgian Malinois. He doesn't like the rain, hates going up the stairs and is noise sensitive which I will go into more detail later.

Finn is a Shepador, Labrador cross with a German Shepherd. He loves food, food and mmm food. He is two and half years old at the time of writing this. He was a nightmare teenager, which inspired me to help frustrated pet gundog owners survive the tricky teenage stage.

The tricky teenage stage is when a cute and well-behaved puppy turns into a rebellious troublemaker. This can last between 6-18 months old in a gundog. The most common teen behaviours that I deal with on a daily basis are jumping up, mouthing, reactivity, pulling on lead and unreliable recall.

I will be covering these behaviours in more detail in book 2, ' *Taming your teenage tearaway*' of the Teenage Pet Gundog Series.

Now, the introductions are over. Let's get back to the fireworks,

I have spent years watching my parent's dogs Barney and Jake being so terrified of fireworks. It really is the worst feeling, being powerless, not knowing how to make them feel better. That is why, when I got Finn, I knew I wanted him to be calm when the bangs go off.

In this book, I will share with you all my secrets on how to stop your pet gundog from being scared of fireworks and how I got Finn calm, relaxed and 'balls in the air' chilled out. You can achieve this too (maybe legs in the air if the vet has taken his balls or if you have a 'she')

Ah, talking about 'she'. It will be really annoying if I kept on saying 'he' and 'she' every time, so to keep things simple so dogs of both sexes will be referred to as 'he'.

There is no point in reading this book and saying 'oh, I enjoyed that' and then shelving it after. At the end of each chapter, there are action points that I want you to go away and take action on.

Take action, and you will get more out of this book, and you will get even more value from this book by having free access to ' *How to stop your pet gundog from being scared of fireworks*' online short course go to:

www.pawtasticgundogadventures.co.uk/teenage-pet-gundog-firework-survival-guide/

Right, that's cleaned that up.

Let's get cracking…

Chapter 1
Fear itself

Many historians believe that fireworks were originally developed in the second century B.C. in ancient Liuyang in China.

It is believed that the first natural "firecrackers" were bamboo stalks that, when thrown in a fire, would explode with a bang because of the overheating of the hollow air pockets in the bamboo.

The Chinese had already discovered that mixing certain chemical substances with fire created smoke of different colours.

These substances were combined with the gunpowder containers to create the combination of a loud bang and brightly coloured smoke that we recognise today as fireworks.

They believed that fireworks could frighten away evil spirits and also provide good luck and happiness.

Today, fireworks are now used to celebrate Bonfire night, New year and various other occasions all year around. This causes many problems for our dogs and other furry neighbours. Many dogs spend their evening being nervous quivering wrecks. Unfortunately, we have to witness them in distress.

According to the PDSA Animal wellbeing report 2019 (PAW), 23 per cent of dog owners said their dog was afraid of fireworks. It is one of the top five behaviours dog owners would like to change.

RSPCA research revealed that 62 per cent of dog owners say their animals are visibly distressed when fireworks are going off.

What to look out for

If your dog is scared, you may notice your dog does one or more of the following;

- Trembling and shaking
- Clinging to owners
- Excessive barking
- Cowering and hiding behind furniture
- Trying to run away or escape
- Going to the toilet in the house
- Lip licking
- Pacing and panting
- Refusing to eat (you know there is something wrong with a Labrador when he leaves his food)
- Destructive behaviour (chewing furniture etc.).

We had a handyman in to fix some bits and bops around the house. At first, I thought Finn, my dog, was fine and was just excited to see a new visitor, but when I really looked and watched his behaviour. I soon realised he was struggling; he started to bark, pant more rapidly and was not settling at all. He was finding this all too much, and I knew I needed to take action fast.

This is why it is important to spend time observing your dog both at home and when you are out. This will help you to become familiar with his body language so that you know what is normal for your dog, and also, you will know when he is acting out of character.

Dogs can't speak to you and say, 'I am scared, please help' they do this by how they behave. It's your responsibility as his owner to learn to read his body language. The earlier that you spot that something is wrong, the quicker you will be able to help him.

This will help you in many other situations like at the park, if he is nervous or not too sure about something. You will be better equipped to deal with the situation.

The same happened when I first started learning how to help my daughter, who has expected autism.

Once, I started to understand her and spot the signs she was about to have a meltdown. I started to have a better relationship with her. The same can happen with your dog.

When you have noticed the signs that your dog is stressed, then write it down on a notepad or put it in the notes on your phone. Do this over a few weeks, and you will get a better picture of what signs to look out for.

Every gundog is different

As with people, the degree of sensitivity can vary between individuals, and it's the same with our dogs. They will also display different responses to fireworks.

My parent's dogs, Jake and Barney, live in the same house and hear the same firework noise but will have different responses to the noise. Barney will try to hide and go upstairs if he is downstairs, trembling and shaking, whereas Jake will run downstairs and look for a way out. I think if we had a door open, he would bolt. And my dog Finn, well he sleeps through it with his balls in the air that's how relaxed he is.

Flight and fight

It's a chilly Saturday Autumn evening. Everyone is settled for the evening hurdled around the television watching Strictly Come Dancing, comfy dressing gown on and waiting for hot chocolate to cool down.

Dogs are chilled out, two upstairs and one flopped out on the sofa, balls in the air and it's oh so quiet'.

Wait for it!

And cue Bjork song 'It's oh so quiet.'

It's oh so quiet

Shh shh

It's oh so still

Shh shh

You're all alone

Shh shh

And so peaceful until

Bang! Bang! Bang!

Then Jake the dog flies down the stairs, panicking and looking for somewhere to hide.

Yep, the sound of the terrible fireworks.

It completely ruins the evening. Everything is interrupted, you have missed one of the Strictly contestants getting a ten, and you now have to deal with a stressed-out dog, and you have to watch him going through hell, and by now, you are pretty pissed off.

What Jake did there was a typical flight response to a fearful situation.

Unfortunately, for your dog, no matter how many times you try to explain the concept of fireworks to him, he just doesn't get it. As far as he is concerned, there are just two options fight and flight.

This 'fight or flight' response causes certain physiological actions in your body. There is a rush of adrenaline, which results in an increased heart rate, rapid breathing, constricting blood vessels, and a tensing of muscles. All in readiness for a fight or a rapid escape. Basically, his body is getting ready for action as if his life depended on it.

In stressful situations, I haven't thought clearly and panicked and took the wrong cause of action.

In flight and fight mode, dogs do not think clearly either, and they behave differently from what they would normally do. That's why dogs choose to escape in stressful situations

Sensory overload

When Scarlett is in the car, if an ambulance or a motorbike comes past, she puts her hands over her ears. People with autism hate loud noises. She is not keen on my singing either, but I think that's for a totally different reason. In Scarlett's own words, 'you don't sound good, mummy'.

Anyway, moving on, Scarlett really struggles to sleep when fireworks are going off. She normally wears ear defenders in bed. Obviously, that is something we can't get our dogs to wear. Things would be a lot easier if you could.

Fireworks can be very loud even for human ears, let alone dogs, as they produces a sound output that is in the 150 to 175 decibel range. That is pretty high. A jumbo jet taking off is about 120 decibels.

They can hear at roughly four times the distance that humans can. This explains why Finn can hear me at the back of the garden when I open a bag of his favourite treats. He comes running up to me and sits by my feet. Also, they are able to detect much higher frequency noises such as those produced by 'silent' dog whistles and sonic noise deterrents.

It doesn't just affect their hearing. They also have a fantastic sense of smell and will be able to detect the various smoke scents in the air. And, although their eyesight is nowhere near as impressive as their hearing and sense of smell, they can still see the bright flashes of light in the sky.

Basically, a dog is bombarded with sensory overload. And it's all telling him to 'fight or flight'.

To comfort or not to comfort

I receive a lot of questions, asking whether owners should comfort their dogs when fireworks are going off. My answer is always yes, but there are a few things to take into account.

Seeing the distress that fireworks can cause your dog can, quite understandably, make you feel stressed, agitated, upset, angry, and just generally pissed off.

However, if at all possible, you should try to keep these feelings to yourself. And I'll tell you why:

Studies have found that the emotions that we display can impact how our dogs behave in stressful situations.

They will also look to us to see how we react to certain situations and take guidance from our responses.

If we scream when a bang goes off, then our dogs will see it as something to be scared of, so it is best to just ignore the bangs.

When Finn hears a bang, he will bark as if to say, 'what's that' then look at me for reassurance.

I smile and tell him, 'it's fine', and then he lays back down balls in the air. I do the same if he barks when he hears someone at the door or a general noise. I say 'thank you'. If I am not bothered, then he is not bothered.

Dogs are very good at reading our body language. He knows if you are sad or happy. This is why I look at him and smile. He knows the bangs are nothing to worry about.

2 week break

I don't know about you, but whenever I have had a stressful point in my life, such as exam pressure or money troubles. I have felt like I needed a rest.

The consistent and ongoing increase in heart rate and the elevated levels of stress hormones can take a toll on the body. It is the same with our dogs during firework season.

The best cause of action is to give your fearful dog two weeks off to recover. After the firework season is over, it is a good idea to try not to do anything that will stress him out, like having a workman in or going to a routine vet appointment.

It's like a doggy holiday, and you can have my permission to take it off as well.

Chapter Summary

- Spot the signs and write them down into some kind of diary.
- Like us, all dogs have different responses to the fireworks.
- We need to bear in mind that dogs behave differently than they would normally when in flight and fight. This is why when dogs hear fireworks, they decide to bolt or try to escape.
- It is okay to comfort and give our dogs reassurance when the fireworks go off.

Action point

Write down any signs of fear that you have spotted?

Think about how you have responded after a bang has gone off.

Could you do anything differently?

In the next chapter, we will be deep diving into the factors of fear. I will see you then.

Chapter 2
Fear factor

Have you ever wondered why some dogs are so calm around noisy environments while others look nervous and stressed?

Some dogs are comfortable with fireworks, some are not. Some dogs learn to associate the fireworks with noisy party people who display strange unsettling behaviour, usually drunk people on New Year's Eve.

It's impossible to predict which dogs will be more likely to develop noise sensitivity. Early experiences and the upbringing of the dog can play a huge role.

If you want your dog to be comfortable with everyday sounds, then you must introduce these sounds to him in the early stages of development. That's why many breeders make a point of banging feed bowls and clapping hands at feeding time to ensure that young puppies associate noise with pleasure.

When I got Finn at eight weeks old, he was scared of my hairdryer. This is the sort of noise I want him to get familiar and comfortable with.

Firstly, I started to play him the hairdryer sound on the Soundproof puppy app on low volume a few times a day and when he started to ignore the noise. I increased the volume, and he is completely calm now, so I can turn on my hairdryer whenever I like.

If you plan on taking your dog to a field for a shoot, then puppies need to be calm and comfortable around a gunshot noise. This introduction must be both gentle and gradual. This will avoid puppies being gun-nervous or gun-shy.

Finn has heard the firework noise from a young age. I did the same thing as I did with the hairdryer noise. He is not bothered about fireworks, whereas poor Jake is a rescue dog. My parents adopted him when he was twelve weeks old, so we have no idea of his past experience. He is scared of fireworks and is noise-sensitive, so this could be a consequence of his restricted early learning.

Gunshot vs fireworks

A shotgun noise is a completely different sound in pitch and frequency to a firework. Just because a dog is fine with one loud noise doesn't mean he will be fine for all bangs.

Gundogs can associate shots with something interesting that is about to happen. They can see the guns getting fired, smell the powder birds dropping and flying. They know it's time to do what they were bred to do.

Whereas fireworks are just lots of noise with no obvious reason, and quite often, gundogs cannot determine where it all comes from, as fireworks take place in the dark. The noises seem to be coming from everywhere, and perhaps most importantly, they can't see what or who is causing all the noise.

It's a bit like watching a scary film like' Scream'. It's scary because you can hear the masked killer, but you have no idea when the masked killer will appear.

Neutering

In 2013, I was a veterinary nurse. One thing that was drummed into me about early neutering was 'neuter, neuter and wait for it… 'neuter', but since becoming a dog trainer, I have realised that early neutering is not always best.

Neutering is very much an emotive subject. Well-meaning- people will happily give their opinions about when you should neuter your dog. Some vets will even encourage pet owners to neuter early.

There is so much pressure for owners to neuter their dogs. I have even heard a pet professional actually give advice to their client to neuter their dog to help with lead pulling. The most unhelpful piece of advice goes to…

Let me put the record straight, you have heard it here first, dear reader, neutering will not improve your dog's behaviour. Only training will do that. Please do not listen to anyone who tells you any different.

You may be thinking, what does this have to do with fireworks? Well, studies have found that dogs that have been neutered early are more likely to have fear and noise phobia.

Jake was neutered early because that is protocol from rescue centres to stop unwanted pregnancies, and Jake is noise-sensitive and scared of fireworks. I do believe that if he had not been neutered so early and had proper early experiences with noise, he would not be so reactive to everything.

You wouldn't neuter your human 16 year old. They need the testosterone to help them mature into the human being they are going to be. It's the same for our dogs.

If you have a young dog around eight months old and you are thinking about neutering. I would wait until they are between two and a half - three years old when the hormone levels are lowered, and they have matured physically and mentally. Especially if they are showing signs of reactivity or fear, they need the confidence that the hormones give them.

If you think neutering is right for your teenage dog, then ask your vet about chemical neutering, which is injecting an implant under the skin to tell the brain not to produce hormones. You could consider this first, then you know whether you are making the right decision because once the balls come off, you can't glue them back on again.

Company

When we start to approach the firework season, I usually make sure Finn is separate from other the dogs Barney and Jake.

This is because dogs learn from other dogs. The last thing I want is Finn learning to be scared of fireworks from the others.

For this reason, you should not consider getting a second dog in the hope that it will help the first one to settle, as very often, he will simply pick up on his fears and then you will have two scared dogs instead of just one.

Second fear stage

Dogs have a second fear period that happens somewhere between 6-14 months of age. Sometimes, this just happens once, but in other dogs, it can happen several times, which may coincide with growth spurts or hormone surges.

During this period, your young dog may be reactive or be scared of things that haven't bothered them in the past, for example, people, dogs, unfamiliar objects or places.

A bad experience at this time can have a lasting effect on your dog's behaviour, even if all their previous interactions have been positive.

A perfect example of this was when Finn was about eight months old and saw a lady on a mobility scooter riding along. He barked, which is very unlike him because we have seen the same woman most days while out on a walk. I smiled at him, said, 'it's fine', and the next time we saw her again, I gave him a treat so he would associate the scooter lady with something good.

The same could happen with fireworks. You may find that he is comfortable with fireworks going off on one day, but the next day or next year, it may be a whole different situation.

Chapter summary

- If you want your dog to be comfortable with everyday sounds, then you must introduce these sounds to him in the early stage of development.
- Dogs learn from other dogs. If you have a multi-dog household, it is likely they will pick up on each other's fears.
- Neutering will not improve your dog's behaviour; only training will do that. Dogs who have been neutered early are more likely to have fear and noise phobia.
- During second fear stage, young dogs may be scared of things that haven't bothered them in the past.

Chapter 3
Pawtastic Survival Checklist

When I was in secondary school, I was rather shy and didn't say boo to a goose. My ambitions were to become a vet and be David Beckham's wife. Unfortunately, both did not happen. I wasn't very good at science, and sadly, Victoria Beckham got there first. Boo... Sad face.

One thing from school, which did stay with me, was how to be organised and well prepared.

My school made a big thing about the Scientist, Benjamin Franklin's quote:

'By failing to prepare, you are preparing to fail.'

I think this is very true, and you can use this quote for everything, including getting ready to go for a walk, as I pretty much carry everything but the kitchen sink in my treat bag. I have treats, tennis ball, poo bags and of course, my many whistles. I wouldn't be a gundog trainer without my whistle.

When I was learning to drive, my instructor taught me a sort of driving checklist to go around a corner; it was check mirrors, slow speed, position and change gear.

If I wasn't prepared, driving around the corner. Probably, I would have ended up crashing into someone's house going too fast. My firework's survival checklist works the same way. To have success, you need to be prepared.

Firework night is definitely one night you need to be prepared for. But unfortunately, bangs seem to go off in as early as October, so I would suggest getting in a routine of doing my 10 point firework survival checklist on the 1st of October or even earlier if you can. Then you will be more successful in helping your gundog.

Here is my 10 point Firework survival checklist to make sure you do everything that you can to make the night as calm as possible.

Pawtastic 10 point Firework Survival Checklist

1. Make sure your dog has updated microchip details and identification tag on a collar

Dogs can react very badly to the unfamiliar sights and sounds of fireworks. In 2017, statistics show that there was a rise in calls to the Petlog lost pet line at the end of October and beginning of November.

My dad took Barney and Jake out on a walk, Jake heard a gunshot in the walks, and he got spooked and bolted. We all went out looking for him. We were so worried.

When you are in that situation, lots of scenarios that can ran through your mind. What if he has crossed the road and got hit by a car, and worst thought of all, what if we never see him again.

Thankfully, Jake had an up-to-date identification tag on his collar. A lovely lady found him and phoned my mum straight away and kept him safe until we could collect him.

I can't stress enough how important it is to make sure your details are kept up-to-date. Currently, Petlog have stated that 53 per cent of microchips have incorrect owner details, meaning that if a pet goes missing around Bonfire Night, many dogs may not be able to be returned to their owners.

A scared dog can wiggle out of their harness and collar even if tightly adjusted, so invest in a well-fitting harness with an adjustable buckle at the front and back.

Should the worst happen and he runs off, it might be wise to contact www.doglost.co.uk, which will be able to help you organise a search and social media posts

2. Go out for a walk earlier than usual.

Try to stick to normal routines as much as possible but saying that when he comes down to walks and feeding time, you may need to do this earlier.

When I am experiencing a stressful time or worried about something, I don't feel like eating. This is the same with your dog when he is scared, so it's a good idea to take him out for a walk earlier and then, after a sufficient amount of time, feed him.

If your gundog has had a good amount of exercise and had a good meal, then he is more likely to just sleep afterward, a bit like me after a Sunday roast and a few pints of Guinness.

Another plus is that exercise releases feel-good chemicals, like serotonin, that will naturally reduce any feelings of stress that your dog may experience.

Try to do all this before it gets dark when the fireworks are likely to start. If you are someone that won't get back from work until 5-6pm, then it will be probably be dark, but in Chapter 4, I will cover how to tire your gundog without taking him out.

Introduce these changes gradually over a few weeks so you don't suddenly disrupt your dog's routine.

3. Don't leave your dog home alone

If you think that when you leave the house, your dog will be happy to be in charge and order a pizza and be like Macaulay Culkin in Home Alone, you are mistaken.

If you go out, he will be far more likely to panic and also react badly if left on his own.

Please do your dog a favour, stay in with your dog and have a pizza (will just you, not him. He can have a chew).

As I am not completely the fun police, there are times you may need to go out, then please ask someone you trust to come and sit with your dog for the evening. Make sure they follow this checklist and your own routine.

Some owners still think it is fine to tie up their dog to a lamp post outside when they are going into a shop. Please don't do this, especially when fireworks are going off and also, your dog may be stolen as dog theft is on the rise.

4. Keep dog flaps, windows, doors, blinds and curtains shut

When I was a child, Max, our family dog, went through a cat flap when he was a puppy, it took him a while to get all his body through the flap, but he did it in the end. It was so funny, I was expecting the cat, but no, it was Max instead. He obviously didn't fancy the back door.

When dogs are scared, they are not thinking rationally, so even though the fireworks are outside, a terrified dog may still attempt to run out or try to get through the cat or dog flap. It was a good idea to shut all exit routes like windows, flaps and doors.

It might be worthwhile to put a sign on your front gate 'keep the gate shut'. I have heard horror stories of visitors leaving gates or doors open. A dog hears a bang and runs out onto the road and gets hit by a car. It is better to be safe than sorry.

By closing the curtains and windows, you are muffling the sound of fireworks.

It's not only the sound of fireworks that can cause distress for your dog. It's also the light and flashes across the sky. Leave lights on indoors to reduce the impact of the flashes too.

5. Lead by example

Animals are highly perceptive and will notice if you're behaving unusually. Following your dog around or by reacting to the bangs may cause them to feel nervous or unsettled.

You can still reassure your pet by playing with their favourite toy, for example, but try to behave as normally as possible. The more you change your behaviour, the more anxious your dog may become.

6. Make sure your garden is as escape-proof as possible

It would be a good idea to make sure your garden is secure with no holes or gaps for him to squeeze through and fences he can't jump over.

7. Build a doggy den

In the build-up to the fireworks, you could build a doggy den. Somewhere safe and quiet, where he will be less likely to hear the fireworks.

You could use his crate if he has been crate trained. Don't shut the door of the crate. Give your dog options to choose where he wants to hide. Maybe even use an old blanket draped over some chairs.

Make it comfortable for him, put things he likes in it. You could add an item of clothing with your scent to comfort him.

You could even recreate the cupboard under the stairs – move over Harry Potter.

You could leave some of his favourite treats, so he sees the doggy den as a good place to be.

You could put a television in the doggy den so he can watch his favourite shows, probably a step too far, dear reader.

He may not be interested in going in at first. Some gentle encouragement may be needed, but if he doesn't want too then don't force him.

8. Keep your dog's drinking bowl topped up.

When dogs are anxious or stressed, they tend to pant quite a lot so don't worry if he drinks more than normal.

9. Teach a toilet cue

One thing we can't predict is when a firework will go off, and you can bet it will happen when he is outside and needs a wee.

You should be safe after 11 pm as it is the curfew on Bonfire night, but there will always be that one idiot who wants to let one more off and the same idiot who likes letting them off during the day.

This is one of those occasions where it will be handy to have taught a wee command or a cue. He can get on with having a quick toilet break and get back in the house.

Teaching a wee cue is simple and useful. It also has other benefits like no longer waiting in the pissing rain for him to do a wee.

So, here goes how to teach a wee cue;

If the bangs have stopped, pop him on a lead just in case a bang goes off, and you can stop him if he bolts, and also, you can be there for reassurance.

I never want to watch a scary film on my own, so don't let your dog go out on his own if he is scared.

Think of a word for the wee cue. Some common ones are 'go toilet', 'go potty', which by the way, I hate. I personally use 'go wee'. You can choose whatever you like 'release your wee' or 'let the wee be with you.' But remember, you will probably be overheard by your next-door neighbour, so 'fucking take a piss' might not go down well.

Every time you see him going to the toilet outside, say your chosen wee cue until he has finished. Give him a yummy treat and lots of praise for being a good boy. Timing is crucial in dog training; make sure you are ready with the treat and give it to him there and then. We want him to make the connection between the action and reward.

Repeat this stage for a few days. What gets rewarded gets repeated. He will soon get the hang of it.

Next, you can introduce saying your wee cue before he is about to go. Make sure you use the verbal cue before he definitely needs to go; otherwise, he won't make the connection between the word and the action.

If you feel you need to go back to the first stage, then do so, this will establish more firmly the association between the wee cue and the action.

After some practice, you will be able to say the word, and it will encourage him to go to the toilet. When he goes 'go', make sure you give him lots of praise to reinforce the behaviour.

Some dogs will just get it, others will need more practice, but practice makes perfect.

10. Put television or the radio on to drown out the noise

You could make him a doggy playlist. He might like 'Hound dog' by Elvis Presley and 'How much is that doggy in the window'.

I am joking, but you do reach a point during Bonfire night that you will do pretty much anything to calm him down.

When I was younger, I kept many pet rats; they were lovely and so intelligent. The only downside to keeping rats was that they just don't live long enough for my liking, as their average lifespan is 2-3 years old.

My pair of rats, Ronnie and Jonny, were really scared of fireworks, so I borrowed my grandad's old Classic F.M. CD that he got free with the Daily Mail Newspaper. I played the cd on my stereo on repeat throughout the evening and night. He worked a treat. They were calm and just slept. I think I was really chilled out by the end of it as well.

When I spent two weeks work experience at my local cattery, the cats that were staying for their holidays were listening to classical F.M. The cats seems very calm, even some of the cats that were not used to being in a cattery.

The stressed rescue dogs at Battersea Dogs & Cats home listen to Classic F.M. to help keep them relaxed and calm.

Your dog might like to listen to some Beethoven or how about some Mozart. He will be able to tell his gundog friends that he has gone all classy.

Action Point

It might be worth putting a letter through all of your neighbours in your area to ask if they could let them know if they are planning on having fireworks so you can prepare your dog.

Obviously, there will be a 'that idiot' neighbour that will ignore it and let off fireworks and not tell you. You just won't send that neighbour a Christmas card and hope Karma reaches them.

There will be a few that will listen and be considerate; sometimes, people surprise you.

Try to aim to do all ten points of the survival checklist and sign up to get free access to ' *How to stop your pet gundog from being scared of firework*' online short course. As part of the course, you will receive a downloadable PDF of Pawtastic 10 point firework survival checklist. You can print it off and put it on your fridge or anywhere else.

To get your free access, go to
www.pawtasticgundogadventures.co.uk/teenage-pet-gundog-firework-survival-guide/

If you have ever wondered how to tire your dog without going for a walk, well, dear reader, all will be revealed in Chapter 4. I will see you there.

Chapter 4
How to tire your dog without going for a walk

During the firework season, I hear more stories on social media about dogs bolting during a walk. I am sure you have seen them as well. Teenage gundog enjoying his walk with his owner, and then some complete muppet sets off a firework at the park. Dog gets out of his harness and runs off scared, looking for somewhere to hide. Poor owner can't find him anywhere.

Sometimes, it is better to be safe than sorry and not go out for a walk. I know we are creatures of habit, and it sounds weird doesn't it not taking the dog for a walk but don't feel guilty.

So you have just got in from work or turned off the computer from working from home. It is dark, and you have made the right choice of not going for a walk just in case he bolts again on Bonfire night, and you are aware that your teenage gundog will probably freak out if he doesn't go out for a walk and drive you nuts. You know, being the high energy gundog that you know and love. What should you do?

You could hire a reliable dog walker that could walk your dog during the day while you are at work, or you could teach some simple trick training and some scent games to tire him out.

I will show you how in just a jiffy. For now, we need to follow and tick off Pawtastic 10 point firework survival checklist from Chapter 3.

So after he has gone out for a wee, hopefully you will have used the wee cue and prepared the house, the doggy den and drawn the curtains.

So while you are finishing that, I will tell you about pet gundog audit. This will help with teaching him the simple trick training.

Pet Gundog Audit

Finding out what your dog loves is so important, once you find this out, your training is transformed. This is why I always send a copy of 'the pet gundog audit to a new client in their welcome pack.

I know it sounds cheesy, but it's a game-changer. You will see what I mean later in this chapter.

To fill out the pet gundog audit, firstly, we would find out your dog's five favourite treats. If you're not sure, compare two different foods by holding some hidden in each hand, for example, chicken in one hand and cheese in the other. Then offer your fists to your dog and see which he chooses first.

Get on the floor and play with your dog to find out his five favourite toys and five places that they liked to be touched. You need to rank them in order out of five, so the first one should be something that they love the most.

I thought it would be useful for me to show you Finn's pet gundog audit.

Here's Finn pet gundog audit

List your dog's five favourite foods

1. Yorkshire Pudding
2. Cooked liver
3. Chicken
4. Gravy bones
5. Kibble

List your dog's five favourite toys – or things he likes playing with. This should include stuff you don't like him playing with but that is still safe, for example slippers

1. Frisbee
2. Tennis ball
3. Mr Fox
4. Slippers
5. Duck

List your dog's five favourite touch points – where he loves being stroked, touched or tickled.

1. Stomach
2. Under his chin
3. Top of his head
4. Ears
5. Back

I know he loves Yorkshire puddings because one Sunday, my mum was cooking a roast. She had laid out eight large Tesco finest Yorkshire puddings on a baking tray, turned her back for a second. Finn decided to get on the kitchen top and nicked five of the Yorkshire pudding and ate them. I was so embarrassed when my mum told me what he had done.

When we are teaching a dog something new, then we would use his number 1 or 2 from our pet gundog audit treat or toy. We use the term 'high-value treat'. This doesn't mean you should rush to Sainsbury's to buy the most expensive chicken or cheese. 'High-value treats' means what he loves the most. It must be high value to him.

Low-value treat would be a 4 or 5; this might be his normal everyday kibble.

We will use 'Pet gundog audit' in Chapter 5 as well.

Gundog games

You should be ready to start setting up some games that will help tire him out and distract him from the noise outside.

First, I am suggesting that you 'give your pet gundog a job'.

No, I haven't gone nuts.

Every member of the household has a job. Why can't your gundog? I train dogs, Scarlett goes to school, bath's and puts her princess dolls to bed.

My dog, Finn, retrieves his Frisbee and occasionally some gundog dummies.

Gundogs were bred for retrieving birds, but these days, they are often loyal companions without their intended jobs to do. So, we need to find other ways to burn off this physical and mental energy, especially when they can't go out for a walk.

Fifteen minutes of mental stimulation is the same as an hour of physical exercise, so don't be guilty if he doesn't go out for a walk. Just make sure you do other things with him

By giving your dog a job to do, does not mean sending him out to do those things he was originally bred to do necessarily or asking him to carry around a gun – just joking.

Giving your dog a job simply means that you are asking him or her to do something for you in order to earn things of value, such as meals, treats, walks, playing fetch, or whatever it is that your dog enjoys and wants. This is your dog's version of payment for working.

You wouldn't work for free neither should your dog. Most dogs are much happier having a job to do so they can earn payment.

'Giving your gundog a job' encourages the natural instinct of a gundog. This is normally searching and retrieving. In the past, Finn, my dog, has struggled to retrieve to my hand.

It is Sunday tradition in our house to have eggs and soldiers for lunch. Once, my daughter dropped a whole eggshell on the floor. Finn went underneath the table to pick up the eggshell in his mouth and give it to me by hand. I was proud as punch.

You can teach gundogs to retrieve anything, such as slippers, socks, keys and phones. You never know when you could be in a situation where this type of training would come in handy. For example, you could have collapsed and need to call for help. You could have your very own assistance dog without knowing.

Receiving job

Start by throwing a toy and getting him to fetch it. You may find your dog drops it at your feet and not by hand. The easy way to get your dog to retrieve by hand is to say the 'give' cue, and if he does so, reward him with a treat. Do this a few times. He will soon learn if I give you the toy, I get a yummy treat.

Searching job

Spaniels have amazing noses. They are often used for searching for drugs and money at airports.

You can recreate this in your home, but please do not go and get drugs just for your dog to find.

You can hide his favourite toys around the house for him to go and find. If you really want to challenge him, you could get an old tennis ball, cut a hole and put a treat into it. This will give him hours of fun.

You could put his kibble in a Tupperware container with a few holes and hide it around the house. You don't need a container. You can just place the treat or kibble around the house. You ask your dog to 'find it'.

What I normally do is, get one of my daughter plastic egg containers that her LOL surprise dolls came in, and I put kibble in it and place it around my living room for Finn to find. He loves it, but dear reader, do me a favour, please don't tell my daughter as I don't think she would approve.

A great brain game is to tear up some old tea towels. Get two parts of the tea towel and plait them. Then place treats or kibble in the ridges of the Plaits. Your dog should enjoy the challenge of finding them. Try to make it easy at first, so he doesn't give up easily. When he finds them, don't forget to verbal praise him.

Trick training games

I am not expecting you and your dog to start trick training and enter yourself into Britain's Got Talent, but anything is possible.

I love trick training, and so does my dog. We do it every day.

In 2020, the United Kingdom went through a national lockdown because of the Covid-19 pandemic. Part of the restrictions was that we could only go for one hour of exercise a day as we normally go for two walks per day.

I was thinking what I am going to do; Finn is going to be very hyper and drive me nuts. Anyway, I did what I had to do, so at about 5pm, I started trick training with him. Surprise, he was tired, and I didn't know the difference to when we go for a second walk.

It is a great bonding activity with your dog, and it helps to distract your dog from other things, for example, birds, squirrels and, of course, fireworks.

Trick training is about guiding your dog into any position you want by using food or treats.

It is always a good idea to play with him for about 5 minutes before learning a new trick, so he is focused on you.

Down

From a sit position, move your hand from your dog's face area. Make sure you have got his attention by holding a treat or toy. Slowly move your hand down towards the floor in front of him and give him the reward.

Tell him he's a good boy or use 'yes' when he does it. Timing is everything. As soon as he does it, then reward him. What gets rewarded gets repeated. That is, if we reward our dog for a certain action or behaviour, then they are more likely to repeat it again in the future in the hope of another reward.

You may find he slides down just a little at first, then always reward your dog for trying.

Stand

You will be glad you taught your dog to stand as it is really handy when you take him to the vets or if your dog needs regular grooming.

This trick can be quite tricky. It is easier if your dog has a reliable sit or a down, so make sure he knows those first.

To teach a dog a stand is simply to guide him into a standing position when he is sitting or lying down in front of you.

Remember to reward him even for attempting to stand.

Touch

Teaching a 'hand touch' is also a good way to improve your timing when teaching tricks. Ideally, you want to be verbally rewarding your dog with a 'good boy' as soon as his nose touches your hand.

The quicker you 'mark' the desired behaviour with some praise, the easier it will be for your dog to understand what you want him to do.

Start by rubbing a treat or kibble on the palm of your hand. Your dog will instantly be drawn to the smell of the food, and bingo, he touches your hand. As soon as his wet nose touches your hand, reward him.

When he gets the idea, you can try it on the other hand.

Rollover

You would need to start this trick from the down position, and take a treat and hold it just in front of his nose, so he stays in a down position. Then slowly move your head with the treat in behind your dog's ear and over the back/top of his head. When he follows the treat, he flops over onto his side.

Some dogs get this trick straight away, but for others, it can take a bit longer.

Spin

Spin is my favourite trick to teach, and the dogs love it.

To do this trick, firstly, you need to sing Kylie Minogue Spinning around repeatedly.

'I'm spinning around, move outta my way'.

I'm joking, but singing is optional.

This trick is easier if your dog is standing up. Hold the reward in front of his face. Your dog should follow your hand and circle round.

This exercise usually takes a little while, and you should definitely be rewarding your dog for doing a quarter turn, then a half and eventually a full turn.

Once your dog has got the idea, you can take the trick further. I play spin and throw with Finn. I ask him to spin, I can put my hand out to signal whether I want him to spin left or right and let him spin a few times, then reward him with a toy. This really does tire him out, and he loves it.

Through the legs

This is another really easy trick, and I like it because it is a fun way to encourage your dog to come back to you.

You can use a toy or treat, which you should first show your dog to get his attention. Place your legs fairly wide apart then either drop a toy or treat just between your legs and reward your dog with lots of praise when he picks it up.

You can also hold the treat in your hand and bend down. Wave the treat, and he should come running between your legs.

There is a danger your dog will have you over, especially if you have a large gundog, so it is a good idea to ask your dog to sit when he is between your legs.

My top tips

When you have repeated the tricks enough times, you can begin to add commands. While your dog is doing the trick, add the command 'spin' when he is doing the spin. Say 'touch' when he is doing the touch. He will pair up the command with the trick and the reward.

In my experience, only reward when you have given the command; otherwise, your dog will just learn to spin or roll over whenever he wants to get a treat!

Once your dog has the hang of it and is regularly following commands, try to guide him into position using your hand and also, you can begin phasing out the treats. Ask him to do a few tricks, then reward.

If he becomes bored or not quite getting the hang of it, then stop, take a break and try again tomorrow. Have a play session instead. Like us, dogs learn better when they are having fun!

Remember, dogs are good at reading body language, so if he does something great, then smile and make sure he knows it.

Kongs and puzzles

Kongs are silly rubber shaped things that have a hole in the bottom where you put the food.

It is important to get the right sizes for your breed, so for gundog likely to be an L or XL.

The beauty of these funny shaped objects is you can stuff the Kong with anything that you like, table leaf overs. To make things more of a challenge, you can pop the Kong in the freezer.

Stuffed Kongs are great for mental stimulation as they have to work out how to get the food out of the Kong.

There are lots of puzzles and treat dispensers on the market. My dog loves them. I have never fed Finn from a bowl. If I did, he would hoover it in one minute, so I want him to use his nose to sniff out the kibble for mental stimulation.

Lick mats are basically plastic mats that you can spread wet food on, but to be honest, it wouldn't last five minutes with a Labrador. I suggested this to a client once, she had a Labrador. He licked it for a bit, then just carried it around in his mouth. Oh well, gave him something to do while doing the Labrador wiggle.

Snuffle mats are a good texture for your dog. You can hide your dog's treats and kibble. They get to use their nose. Sniffing is very calming for dogs, so this is even more important during Bonfire night.

You can even do DIY puzzles; you can be as creative as you like. You can wash out and take the top of an empty milk container and put kibble in that and enjoy watching him have fun, and don't be surprised if he carries it around.

You can put kibble in cardboard tubes then put it in an Amazon box with all the cardboard wrapping. Cardboard boxes are great fun for dogs, but I must stress that if you do allow your dog to rip up boxes, he might start ripping up boxes that you don't want him to like at Christmas and certain vibrating toys in boxes. Wink wink, ladies.

Some dogs find chewing soothing. This helps to calm them down when they are anxious. Similar to us, when we fiddle with our hair and why children suck their fingers and dummies.

You can give your dog a long-lasting chew, such as a marrow-bone on the dreaded firework night. Finn's personal favourite chew is a good quality meat stuffed in a cow hoof. This gives him hours of fun and relieves boredom.

Chapter Summary

- It is important to find out what your dog loves by using 'the pet gundog audit'.
- We need to give our dog's mental stimulation as well as physical stimulation.
- Trick training and 'giving your gundog a job' will not only tire them out, but also it will improve your relationship with your dog.
- Sniffing is really calming for dogs, so during the firework season, provide your dog with scent games.

Action point

Pick one or two tricks to start with and practice them.

Dogs learn by repetition, so do them over and over again.

Don't forget to praise him!

It is difficult to know what to do without someone showing you, so with that in mind, I have included 'how to' videos that will show me demonstrating all the trick training which you will get from the ' *How to stop your pet gundog from being scared of firework* ' online short course.

All you need to do to get access to this free training is go to www.pawtasticgundogadventures.co.uk/teenage-pet-gundog-firework-survival-guide

Next, we will be focusing on some simple training that will change how your dog sees fireworks. You won't want to miss this. I will see you on the next page.

Chapter 5
Desensitisation

Dear reader, Are you a fan of the T.V. American sitcom Friends?

I know, silly question, you probably are; otherwise, we can't be friends.

Just kidding.

Do you remember the episode, 'the one with the Hypnosis tape' where Rachel can't stand Chandler smoking anymore? Rachel hands him a hypnosis tape her friend used to play, which helped her quit smoking. Chandler starts playing it every night, and the results are successful, as he stops smoking.

Wouldn't it be good if we could just hand a hypnosis tape to our dogs to stop them from being scared of fireworks? If only.

However, we do have the next best thing –Desensitisation. This is the process that aims to help your dog overcome his fears by exposing him gradually to the sound recordings of firework noises.

The desensitisation process should be performed well in advance of any real fireworks events; otherwise, the sound of the real fireworks may still scare your dog and risk undoing the benefits of the therapy.

How desensitisation works

My daughter, Scarlett, likes to wear her yellow Belle dress (the one from Beauty and the Beast) and bring all of her Disney princesses downstairs.

Then she asks 'Alexa' to play 'Wham', and she dances with her princesses in the living room. She loves watching her reflection on the television when it is turned off. If you want to watch television in our house, you are a bit out of luck.

It always must be 'wham, and nothing else will do. She asks me to play it in the car as well. She thinks George Michael is very pretty and would like to marry him. My heart sank when I had to tell her that, actually, George Michael is in heaven.

I am sure your dog would prefer some George Michael's songs as well, but if we are going to overcome his fear of fireworks, instead, we will need to put some firework sounds on for him.

I would start by playing firework sounds on your phone at low volume to see how he responds.

You can get firework sounds from YouTube, Alexa, and the Dogs trust have a downloadable 'sounds scary' page visit https://www.dogstrust.org.uk/help-advice/dog-behaviour-health/sound-therapy-for-pets .

Personally, I have used the 'Soundproof puppy training' app, which you can get from iTunes.

It has got everyday sounds that you would want your puppy to be comfortable with, such as hairdryer, drilling to baby crying, and of course fireworks

When Finn was a puppy, I played him every sound, especially the firework sound when he was sleep, eating and when I played with him.

He associates great things (food and playing) with those sounds. He is not bothered by fireworks at all. He's calm and lies down with his balls in the air.

This is my simple step to step method that helped me have a calm dog for the firework season.

Stage 1

I would like you to refer back to your Pet Gundog Audit and look at what you put down as your dog's top favourite treat.

Start with your chosen firework noise on your phone at a low volume level. Try to do this for 20-30 seconds initially to see how your dog responds.

Take some time to observe your dog's behaviour. If he is comfortable at the starting volume, then slowly, after three sessions, begin to increase the volume. You want to find the sweet spot where your dog is clearly aware of the noise but is not showing signs of being stressed or scared.

You may find it useful to make a note of the volume level so that you can ensure that you start at the right level on your next session.

Short and regular session is best. I would aim to play the sounds at the chosen volume level for 5-10 minutes at a time and ideally a couple of times a day. Remember that you must be calm and relaxed throughout the process as your dog may look to you for guidance.

When you are playing the sounds, give him treats. This is to help your dog have a positive association with the sound of fireworks.

To get the best results, I would use high-value treats, so when a firework sound goes off, you need to be ready with a juicy piece of chicken (or whatever your dog's favourite treat is, refer back to your pet gundog audit).

Be prepared to use a lot of treats, and you need to give him one after the other.

If you are worried that your dog will become overweight, you could use cooked chicken or liver so you can easily break tiny pieces.

As the training progresses, you wouldn't need as many treats as you did when you first started. You will gradually fade them out when your dog is more comfortable when the fireworks go off.

Food is more effective because of the direct positive pleasure effect of food on the brain. It helps the dog's brain link to positive emotions with the previously scary thing, so they eventually see the scary thing as good.

From now on, as far as your dog is concerned:

LOUD BANG = FANTASTIC TREAT

Here, you want your dog to look to you for guidance and reassurance. If he sees that you are happy and relaxed, then he will be too.

Once you are happy that your dog's reaction to the noises has reduced, you can consider moving to stage 2.

Stage 2

This stage is about creating the most realistic firework noise. You can do this by setting up a sound system with speakers.

Place the speakers in different positions in a room to make sure your dog doesn't associate the noises as always coming from the same place.

Make sure that you leave the door open so that your dog can leave if it feels the need to.

This will be a gradual process, and it will take a number of weeks of daily training.

It is very difficult to tell you how long until your dog will show significant improvement. It depends on the individual dog. It is important to go at your dog's pace. If your dog seems scared, then turn the volume down.

When your dog seems comfortable with stage 2, you can apply what you have learnt in a real firework situation. Remember to be calm and relaxed , hear a loud bang and then give treat.

Keep up the training even if you think you have cracked it. Something may have happened like an unexpected event (second fear stage, as I mentioned in Chapter 2), or he may hear a strange noise and may have to go back a stage, so it's crucial you carry on with this training. I still do this with Finn, especially when it is the lead up to the firework season.

Fitting training into your daily life

In August 2020, during the coronavirus pandemic, I began to have the lockdown flab, and I decided I wanted to feel good about myself and have a toned stomach. I have never been happy with the way I looked. I wanted to feel more confident, so I went on a fitness journey.

I would schedule 30 minutes a day for my fitness workout. This is a manageable length of time, and I am able to stick to it.

If I decided to schedule an hour in, do you think I would stick to it and fit it in around everything else?

Probably not.

It's the same with dog training; you have to be able to fit it into your life; otherwise, you won't be able to keep to it. When I am working with a new client, I always think about how training will fit in with their lifestyle. I think about 'how much time do you have' depending on the answer. This helps me create their tailored training plan, and more likely, it will help get them results.

The beauty of this type of training is you only need 5 – 10 minutes per day. It is better than one long session per week. You could play some fireworks sounds while waiting for your dinner to cook or even when it's the advert break on your favourite television programme.

Getting started is the hard part, but making it a daily habit is even harder. Tell your family and friends what you are going to do and commit to it. I can guarantee you will need help and support because it can be difficult to keep going with the training. You might forget one day, then it turns into two, then three, and weeks start to go by. Life does get in the way.

Often if you are specific with a task, you will make it more manageable, so rather than say, "I'm going to help my dog be less fearful with fireworks", say "I'm going to spend 5 minutes doing the training during the advert break of Coronation Street". Approaching it in this way will help you set up a daily habit and more likely do the training and get results just like my fitness routine. I have the toned stomach that I have always wanted.

Results don't happen overnight; I didn't do one fitness workout or one trip to the gym and leave with a toned stomach; it took dedication and being consistent every day.

Talking of being consistent, I am going to share with you my 'tame your teen' formula. I will explain all.

'Tame your teen' formula

You are about to learn something rather special. I only teach this formula to my clients. You must not tell anyone, dear reader.

Dog training doesn't need to be complicated. I am a woman of simple brain. I like making things simple as possible.

I am guessing you have heard of CPR. At least, I hope you know what CPR stands for. It is cardiopulmonary resuscitation. It is an emergency life-saving procedure that is done when someone's breathing or heartbeat has stopped.

Now, forget that. I will give you my own version of CPR. I use this formula with all different types of training. It can be used for sound therapy that I have just shown you and also for the trick training in Chapter 4.

Here it is and now remember this is our little secret, so keep it to yourself.

Consistent

By rewarding the same good behaviour over and over again, your dog will learn quicker.

Every time a bang goes off, you are ready with the chicken or his favourite treat.

Persistent

There are no quick fixes in training, just keep on trying.

Repetition

Like us, all dogs learn through repetition.

If you follow this formula, you won't go far wrong, and you will have effective results.

Chapter summary

- Desensitisation can be used to help overcome your dog's fear.
- It must be performed well in advance before real firework events.
- It is important to go at your dog's pace.
- You need to be able to fit 5 minutes of training into your daily life-style to achieve effective results.

Action point

I would love you to start with stage 1 of the training today.

Just remember, it's just 5 minutes per day—the amount of time the average microwave meal takes. I will leave that thought with you!

Let's move on to alternative remedies.

Chapter 6
Alternative Remedies

Your dog is shaking in the corner, and you are at your wit's end. Bang, bang and bang are all you can hear.

Please do not worry, dear reader. There are many ways in which you can help your scared gundog.

You will find some that I mention here may work better than others. It's not a 'one size fits all' type of solution. You may need to use a few remedies at the same time to get the desired result but try not to overwhelm your dog by trying too much at once. Start by trying one or two things at a time and review progress in 2-3 weeks. Then try another one.

Warning, I know I must sound like a broken record but preparation is the key here, as I explained in Chapter 2.

Many of these remedies need to be in place a good few weeks before the fireworks season starts for them to have any kind of benefit.

Calming supplements

There are many calming remedies on the market. It is very much about trial and error and what works for your gundog.

When I worked at the vet's, I was a cat fosterer. I say that now, but I basically took home all the stray cats that found themselves at the surgery. I don't think my parents were too pleased. The common saying was ' *another cat Harriet*'.

When you settle a new cat in your home, they have to become familiar with the new environment, new smells and new everything.

One Friday, I gave a home to a very nervous cat. One of the vets introduced me to Zylkene capsules. He said just sprinkle it over the cat's food, and this will make him feel more relaxed.

I was like, yeah, right.

Like that's going to work. The nervous cat, Fred, was freaking out at every noise. He didn't get the nickname Freaking Fred for nothing.

Anyway, I took the vet's advice, and it worked; after a few days, he started to chill out, which did relax me. You always worry when you bring home another pet and think to yourself, *'have I done the right thing.'*

There was a happy ending. In the end, he was the best mouse catcher in all of Croydon.

Zylkene contains a natural ingredient derived from a protein in milk called casein that has clinically proven calming properties to help relax cats and dogs.

It is a peptide (protein) molecule, well known to promote the relaxation of newborns after breastfeeding by delivering 'calming messages' to the brain via the body's natural 'messenger.

This is something you could possibly try. You would need to know the weight of your dog to prescribe the right dose, so do seek advice from a vet.

Medication

Vets can prescribe a number of different medications to help calm a frightened dog during fireworks, such as diazepam or a general sedative.

Diazepam is better than a sedative because it blocks memory, so the dog cannot remember being frightened – this means that your dog's fear will not get any worse. However, it is not a strong sedative, so your dog may appear a little more unsettled than with a sedative. The use of DAP plug-in diffuser, which I will cover next, may help settle your dog.

To ensure diazepam will be a suitable medication for your dog to take throughout the firework season, the vet will give your dog a thorough health examination and prescribe a test dose. A small number of dogs given diazepam will show side effects.

Your vet will request that a low test dose be given at a time when you can keep your dog inside and supervised for at least 3-4 hours. The effects of the drug last for about 4 hours, and you should see very little effect on your dog's behaviour. Any apparent side effects should be reported to the vet.

Adaptil (DAP)

What the heck is DAP?

I hear you say.

DAP stands for Dog Appeasing Pheromone.

ADAPTIL is the synthetic copy of the natural "dog appeasing pheromone" released by the mother dog 2-3 days after giving birth. This pheromone comforts and supports her puppies and has been proven to have a comforting effect on both puppies and adult dogs during stressful situations like fireworks.

It is odourless, with no sedative effect and can be safely used alongside medications.

Adaptil comes in many forms, either a collar, spray or plug-in diffuser. This diffuser works like an air freshener plugin.

For the DAP products to work effectively, plug in the diffuser in the room where your dog spends the most time and use it for at least two weeks before the firework event. The diffuser will last for about one month, and you can buy a refill to replace the used one.

When I worked at the vet's, some owners said that it worked really well for their dog. However, I have had other owners say they didn't see any change to their dog.

While using the diffuser, you can apply the Adaptil spray to the doggy den or bedding. After spraying, allow 15 minutes before your dog sits on the bedding or doggy den. The effect only lasts for around 2-3 hours.

You might have to play musical beds with your dog so you can spray the bed again.

Let's move on to clothing that can help.

Calming caps or thunder caps

These are odd-looking hats that fit over and around a dog's head, including the ears. It does look very much like a blindfold for your dog. Ooo kinky.

They calm the dog by reducing the amount of visual stimulation, which when used properly, can be a great aid for fireworks.

They are commonly used for dogs who can get hyper-aroused by car rides but can be used for noise-sensitive dogs.

You can use this with thunderShirt, if you feel more calming is needed.

Anxiety Coats

Many dogs take comfort from tight-fitting clothing. I'm not talking about the canine equivalent of Rylan Clark-Neal in eye-wateringly tight jeans – although perhaps dogs find this amusing too.

The thunderShirt is a snug-fitting coat that helps to calm dogs by applying gentle, even pressure around the dog's body. It is believed that the pressure helps release calming hormones. Similar to swaddling a crying baby or hugging a distressed person. It also helps separation and travel anxiety.

If your dog finds it a comfort to be cuddled, then this might work, but if your dog hates being hugged, then it's probably best to skip this one.

Thundershirt have helped over 80 per cent of cases. These should be introduced gradually. It is secured using Velcro straps. I know some dogs react to the noise of the Velcro, so extra steps need to be made when putting it on. If the sound is all too much for him, then you can use body wrap (which I will into later).

For thunderShirt to be effective, you must get the correct size of your dog; otherwise, it is pretty pointless. It must be snug as a rug.

It is best to put the thunderShirt on before it gets dark and not think, 'oh, there's bang, and I better put it on'.

Once your dog is comfortable wearing it, it can be worn for as long as required, although you should not leave him unsupervised. Also, it can help with separation and travel anxiety.

Body wraps

Body wraps help your dog to feel calmer during these stressful situations. You can actually use a bit of fabric to create a "swaddle" of sorts to help your dog with their anxiety.

Wrap your dog before you most expect them to experience the fireworks and the hug-like effect that soothes the dog, decreasing anxiety. I suggest using a scarf (length depending on the size of the dog) or a stretchy fabric like a bandage.

Simply place the centre of the scarf or bandage across the dog's chest and cross the ends over the shoulders. Next, cross those end beneath the chest and bring back up, tying in a secure knot away from the spine.

Like any piece of training equipment, your dog must be happy to wear it. Think back to when your dog was a puppy. You would let your puppy get used to wearing a collar or harness in the home before wearing it outside. This is the same with a thunderShirt, and the body wraps. If you decide to put it on for the first time on firework night, this could add to your dog's stress rather than help them.

I would recommend putting on these types of clothing many times before firework season in stages and giving treats, so your dog associates wearing the clothing has a good thing.

Tellington TTouch

Tellington TTouch method is one of the most effective ways of helping our pets cope and overcome their fear of fireworks.

The method is based on circular movements of fingers and hands over the entire body to target certain pressure points in the dog's body.

You can learn and do this in the comfort of your own home. However, it may be better to seek advice from a Tellington TTouch Practitioner.

Here are a few reasons why;

When dogs are in a stressed state, they are more likely to bite, especially if you touch a part of the body that they don't like. It's a good idea to refer back to the pet gundog audit in Chapter 4 and look at your dog's top five favourite touch points

You need to be able to read your dog's body language, if your dog is not comfortable with what you are doing, then it is not pleasurable, so there would be no benefit to your dog.

In 2017, I walked a lovely German Shepherd, Roxy, who was reactive to dogs and sometimes towards people. She would bark, mainly because she was scared.

When she would get very scared, I would calm her down by placing the palm of my hand on her shoulder blades and move my hand in a circular motion. I placed hardly any pressure. This was like a Zen moment. She would calm down after 5 minutes of me doing this.

Honestly, I had no idea what I was doing, but it worked. I know now that was a type of TTouch.

I often use this chest rubbing on my dog to calm him down when he is hyper or worried about something.

Chapter Summary

- Some of these alternative remedies may work better than others.
- You may need to use a few remedies at the same time to get the desired result but try not to overwhelm your dog by trying too many at once.
- These remedies need to be in place at least a month before the firework season starts.

Action point

Have a look at the remedies that I have mentioned, pick a few that might work best for your dog.

Harriet's Final Thought

Yay, I am pleased to tell you after six chapters, you have almost reached the end of this book.

Just a few things to tie up before I leave you.

I think you would agree with me, how much our dogs have comforted us when we were sad and unhappy during the Covid -19 pandemic. Our dogs have kept us sane and kept our spirits up.

During the firework seasons, it's our turn to re-pay the favour. This is the time when our dogs need us.

I know how frustrated you are that fireworks are going off and you feel that you can't help him.

Fears can be overcome. However, getting started is the hard part. It will take time and some dedication from you.

I can't guarantee all your dog's fears will go away instantly after reading this book, but you will see changes, and you will definitely have a better relationship with him.

What I can guarantee is that if nothing is done, these fears will get worse unless you do something to address them.

It can be difficult to give general advice without seeing the dog, every dog is different, and that's why I like to tailor my training packages to the dog and their owner.

If you are unsure about how to carry out this training because getting it wrong can make things much worse, then please don't suffer in silence and ask for professional help from a dog trainer or behaviourist.

Hopefully, you are going to sign up for my ' *How to stop your pet gundog from being scared of fireworks*' free online short course. You can gain access by using this link **www.pawtasticgundogadventures.co.uk/teenage-pet-gundog-firework-survival-guide/** which will add more meat to the bones, but you may benefit from getting 1-2-1 training help with me the 'Teenage Gundog Tamer'.

You can have a look at all of my 1-2-1 training packages that I offer by going to

https://pawtasticgundogadventures.co.uk/1-2-1-teenage-training-packages/

Don't worry if you don't live locally, I can still find a way of giving you the help you need. Any questions, please feel free to email me at **info@pawtasticgundogadventures.co.uk.**

A special gift for you

I hope you have enjoyed reading this book, but most of all, I hope it inspires you to take action.

There is only so much you can take away from a book, especially if you are a visual learner like me. I learn much better when it is demonstrated to me, so that's why I have decided to share with you a special gift from me to you, to me to you. I have gone a bit like the Chuckle brothers there.

Anyway, I am giving you free access to ' *How to stop your pet gundog from being scared of firework*' online short course. This free dog training will help you immediately put into practice everything you have learnt in this book.

In this course, you will receive;

- A step by step guide on how to desensitise your dog, so he is more comfortable when fireworks go off.
- A downloadable PDF version of Pawtastic 10 point firework survival checklist.
- How to tire your dog out without leaving the house using trick training.
- How to play the 'find it' game to keep your pet gundog calm and relaxed.

To get your FREE access to this 'must see' training go to:

www.pawtasticgundogadventures.co.uk/teenage-pet-gundog-firework-survival-guide/

About the Author

Harriet Goodall started her career as a paralegal after finishing her law degree in 2010. This wasn't really for her, as she decided to swap her smart legal suits for a fur-covered green uniform.

She had always dreamt of getting into the veterinary profession. Harriet left the solicitor firm to be a veterinary receptionist and later trained to be a veterinary nurse.

In 2013, she found out she was pregnant and gave birth to Scarlett. As you know, when you have children, your priorities change. She wanted to be a hands-on mum, so when Scarlett was six months old, she made the brave decision to start her dog adventure business 'Pawtastic Gundog Adventures'.

Harriet wanted to provide a reliable and trustworthy service for pet owners where they could go to work or go away on holiday and not stress about leaving their pet.

When Harriet was growing up, she fell in love with her parent's dog, Barney. She played and trained him. He is a lovely natured dog. He does the 'lab bum wiggle' whenever he saw her. When she moved out of her parent's home, Barney was the only one that missed her, so she missed him. That's why she got her very own dog 'mini-Barney', Finn. He is Labrador cross with a German Shepherd (Shepador). Harriet and Finn go on their own adventures every day.

In 2019, she followed her passion for gundogs after spending time with the lovely Claire and John Denyer from Family dog services in Maidstone in Kent, which inspired her to help Pet gundog owners.

After enjoying the challenge of training Finn, Harriet decided to become a dog trainer with help from the Marvellous Carol Clark ' *The Doggy Doctor*' from Down dog training Academy.

Finn was a complete nightmare when he was going through the tricky teenage stage. He was jumping at everyone he met, mouthing, lead pulling, and recall was non-existent. She felt like a failure and quickly found training strategies that worked for her and Finn.

Now, she successfully helps many frustrated Pet Gundog owners in simple and practical steps using her own '*tame your teen*' formula. Dog training doesn't need to be complicated, and she is known as the 'Teenage Gundog Tamer'.

Harriet's mission in life is to help and support frustrated pet gundog owners through the tricky teenage stage, so owners do not have to resort to the heart-breaking decision to rehome their dog.

Harriet is known for having a wicked sense of humour and for being controversial and outspoken in all aspects of dog training.

In her spare time, if she is not training her own dog at her home in Croydon or looking after Alan, the guinea pig. She can be found watching Formula 1 while enjoying a pint of Guinness.

If you would like to find out more about '*The Teenage Gundog tamer*', please visit **www.pawtasticgundogadventures.co.uk**

Acknowledgements

Yay Finito.

It took me longer than expected to write and publish this book. One of my many ambitions in life was to become an author. It was so important to me to make sure everything was just right. Call me Goldilocks.

Anyway, firstly I would like to say a massive thank you to my dog training mentor, the lovely Doggy Doctor 'Carol Clark' who has taught me so much. If I am half the dog trainer she is, I will be a very happy bunny. Also, Carol kindly saved the day by illustrating the picture on my front cover. There are no limits to her talents. I absolutely love my book cover now.

Thank you to the 'Pet Biz Wiz', Dominic Hodgson, for all your support, encouragement and for helping me to think big.

Thank you so much to my beta readers, who gave me some great feedback on my book even though I thought it was a bag of shit.

Thank you to Pedro for the creation of the 'Teenage gundog' character on the cover.

Special thanks to Steve for all your support, as always.

Thank you to my Princess Scarlett, who is seven years old at the time of writing this. You are my world and the reason for everything I do.

Many thanks to all of my clients for their loyalty, recommendations and for letting me spend time with their beloved pets. I love getting your progress emails, it makes me so happy, 100 per cent job satisfaction like no other.

I would like to dedicate this book to the stars of the show Jake, Barney and Finn. I couldn't have written this book without all three of you!

Sadly, Barney passed away when this book was in the final stages of editing. He was the most kind and loving dog. He would not hurt a fly. We miss him terribly.

To my buddy, life is so much better with you, Finny.

And a big thank you to you, yes, you dear reader, for taking the time to read this book. I hope it made you laugh, but above all, I hope it makes the dreaded firework season more manageable for you and your dog. If you got any value from this book, please leave me a nice review on Amazon. I would really appreciate it!

Keep retrieving
Harriet
Your Teenage Gundog Tamer.

Printed in Great Britain
by Amazon

85263613R00037